Learn to Win Arguments and

20 Powerful Techniques to Never Lose an Argument again, with Real-life Examples.

A Life Skill for Everyone.

VISHAL GUPTA

OTHER BOOKS BY THE AUTHOR

HIGH on LIFE

ARE YOU DEPRESSED STRESSED UNHAPPY NERVOUS ANXIOUS PANICKY?

A Personal Account of How I Beat Depression of 7 years. 20 Powerful Activities to Uplift your Mood Instantaneously. Never feel Depressed Again. Invest in your Mental Health. Do not live in Denial.

THERE IS NOBODY MORE IMPORTANT THAN YOU!

VISHAL GUPTA

https://vishal-gupta.com/high-on-life

GRAB YOUR FREE GIFT

I am honored and excited to know that you have purchased this book and that you have invested your hard-earned money and given your precious time to this book.

As an act of appreciation and gratitude, I would like to offer you a FREE GIFT:

Click below to Download a free copy of my book "TOXIC PEOPLE."

This book has transformed the lives of thousands worldwide, and I am sure it will also be useful to you.

So, what are you waiting for?

GRAB YOUR FREE COPY BY CLICKING ON THE LINK BELOW:

http://vishal-gupta.com/freebook

TOXIC PEOPLE

...rn to Identify 12 Types of
...Negative Personalities.
...rstand How to Handle such
Characters.
G... edom from Energy Vampires.
Yo... e is Precious. Protect it against
TOXIC PEOPLE.

V...HAL GUPTA

THE BEST WAY TO WIN ANY ARGUMENT IS TO AVOID IT. THE 2ND BEST WAY IS TO READ THIS BOOK.

AUTHORS NOTE

This book is the result of my 30 years of observation, analyses, and experience.

My life has been anything but perfect. I have been through numerous successes and failures. Several ups and downs. Some tremendous accomplishments and some very massive disasters. This has given me a peerless set of experiences that I bring into all my writings and books. Throughout my life, I have made it my mission to share my experiences with as many people as possible.

Language and words cannot be the tongue of soul and say everything. They have limitations. Most misunderstandings, quarrels, and disagreements happen due to the inability of oral and written human language to convey every piece of information and emotion that human beings want to express. The choice of words and tone are very important. Even though the main focus of this book is arguments, in some places, it goes beyond arguments, words, and logic. It explores the human aspect of tone and intention. If this book is read well and understood in its entirety, the reader will improve his relationships and friendships, leading to a happier and healthier life.

Vishal Gupta

Table of Contents

INTRODUCTION 10

TECHNIQUE 1: REPEAT AND REPEAT AND REPEAT. 20

TECHNIQUE 2: SILENCE SPEAKS 25

TECHNIQUE 3: AGREE, DISAGREE 30

TECHNIQUE 4: PRAISE, DISAGREE 35

TECHNIQUE 5: FAULTY PRESUMPTIONS 40

TECHNIQUE 6: STATISTICS AND EXPERT OPINION 44

TECHNIQUE 7: TWO WRONGS ~~DON'T~~ MAKE A RIGHT 48

TECHNIQUE 8: DISCLAIMER 53

TECHNIQUE 9: APPLES VS ORANGES 58

TECHNIQUE 10: AD-HOMINEM ATTACK 63

TECHNIQUE 11: ANGER, ANGER, GO AWAY! 68

TECHNIQUE 12: PROVERB 73

TECHNIQUE 13: LOADED WORDS 78

TECHNIQUE 14: EMOTIONAL VERSUS LOGICAL 85

TECHNIQUE 15: CONDITION FIRST 88

TECHNIQUE 16: SEEK AND YOU SHALL FIND- FAULTY LOGIC 92

TECHNIQUE 17: MAKE A WAGER 97

TECHNIQUE 18: ASK QUESTIONS 100

TECHNIQUE 19: MAJORITY WINS 104

TECHNIQUE 20: SELF DEPRECATION AND SARCASTIC LAUGHTER 108

YOUR RATINGS AND REVIEW MATTER 116

EPILOGUE 118

DEDICATION 121

DISCLAIMER 122

COPYRIGHT © 2020 VISHAL GUPTA 124

Introduction

At the outset, it is essential to define the word **'Argument'** and also contrast it with the word **'Discussion'** so that all of us are on the same page.

Usually, the word argument has a negative connotation and is associated with a loud voice, yelling, anger, and with other such negative emotions. However, that is not entirely true.

In this book, I have used the term 'Argument' in the context of a **'Disagreement'** between two people or two parties where both parties defend and standby their point of view and try to convince the other side of their perspective or try to show how the other's standpoint is not correct. The **intention** in an argument is to show the Opponent how you are **Right** and and how W**rong** the other is.

In **Contrast**, a discussion is a **Conversation** between people to meaningfully talk about a situation, a person, or an event to understand the same thing from various viewpoints without trying to defend a particular person's perspective and without the intention of winning the conversation and having the last word and proving oneself right and the other wrong.

On an average, we get into some kind of disagreement or argument **around 5-6 times** a day.

Sometimes we are in disagreement or argument with our **PARENTS,** whom we respect a lot, but, at the same time, we want to **live our own life on our terms**. Therefore, disagreement and argument become an essential part of our conversation because we want to follow our own path and growth rather than their ideas of what is right for us.

Sometimes we get into disagreements or arguments with our **SPOUSES,** whom we love and care. But at the same time, we **need our space**, and we need to do things which make us happy even if our spouses can't understand us. Unfortunately, in any relationship, it is quite normal for people to **control each other**. Sometimes our spouses may control us to a point where we can't even breathe, and we find it difficult to do activities or chores which make us happy and keep us sane and satisfied. It therefore becomes vital to **win disagreements or arguments** against our spouses for our sanity and joy. We all need our '**Me time**,' our own private time, and our own space.

Sometimes we get into arguments with our **FRIENDS**. Some friends only pretend to be friends. They are not our well-wishers. At the first opportunity they get, they put us down; **ridicule us**, especially in bigger groups. They insult us, directly, indirectly, and demolish everything we say or express. They treat us like dirt. In such situations, it becomes essential to give it back to them. It becomes crucial to win conversations and disagreements or arguments against them. It becomes vital to identify the **various argument techniques** they use to win arguments against us and then counter them, with our knowledge of argumentation styles and structures to demolish their arguments and **prevail over them**. We need to do this sometimes to win back our self-esteem, pride, and **self-confidence**.

Sometimes we are in an argument with our **BOSSES**. 'THE BOSS IS ALWAYS RIGHT' mindset may not always work. There are critical situations when we have to stand up for our views and opinions. Many times, the boss acts **illogically and unreasonably** by misusing **authority**. In such cases, we need to counter his/her outrageous behavior in a way that we can be heard, and our ideas and opinion can be considered. At the same time, we may not want to sound disrespectful or aggressive against him or even tep on their toes. Therefore, it becomes important to know how to argue successfully against authority without hurting the other person's EGO.

Sometimes we are in an argument with our **RESPECTED ELDERS**. They may be our grandparents, relatives, brothers and sisters, etc. In many cultures, arguing against elders is **seen as impolite**. But, in many situations, we have no option but to be heard and to have our way. If we don't argue, it may affect **our whole life and career**. So, how arguing respectfully and tactfully becomes **an art and a science**.

Sometimes, we are in an argument with **STRANGERS** or people we don't know perfectly well and who are harming us by being very aggressive or disrespectful. We find many such people in the trains, buses, malls, and other public places. In such situations, it becomes crucial to successfully win arguments against them to get our work done or our point across to them.

Sometimes, we are in an argument with our **CHILDREN**. Children can be brilliant and tricky. They understand **emotional blackmail** and manipulate elders effectively. Many times we fall into their trap even though it may be harmful to the child. We must learn how to checkmate children in their games and prevail over their emotional blackmail laden arguments for their own safety, security, and wellbeing.

At times, we are arguing with our **EMPLOYEES**. Employees can be challenging and stubborn. When employees make a group and argue, they can be quite effective even though they may be wrong. They may refuse to see the viewpoint of the manager or the employer, and they may argue without being reasonable. In such situations, getting our viewpoint across to them and holding our ground against all their grounds becomes important for our survival and sustainability.

Occasionally, we are amid a high energy, high octane **DEBATE**, either on stage, tv discussion, debate or just amongst friends, associates, relatives. This usually happens during discussions about sensitive topics such as politics, religion, and spirituality. In such debates, there are many people, all having different points of view and all wanting to prevail over the rest to prove their case as right. These people may be loud, aggressive, egoistic, and sometimes even abusive. In such situations, it becomes imperative to argue with extreme care and alertness so that you may get heard; you may speak your mind without stepping on **someone's EGO** or pride. Otherwise, you may land losing friends and relatives to your disadvantage.

This book introduces the reader to 20 practical and powerful **time tested techniques to win** arguments under all the various situations mentioned herein.

There is **no one rule** or principle which fits all situations. Different situations require different solutions. It is on a case to case basis. This book, therefore, introduces the reader to 20 different styles and structures of arguments which can be successfully employed depending on the situation. The readers can use the various techniques mentioned in this book in two ways:-

1) By preventing themselves from falling trap to an opponent, who is using a particular **style and structure** of the argument (by identifying that style of argument and countering it)

2) By successfully using the various techniques and styles of arguments mentioned in this book **against any person, anytime, anywhere.**

Furthermore, before we get into the thick of the topic, some things must be understood in general about the **world or arguments** to appreciate this topic better.

We live in a **world of duality**. There is no absolute right or wrong, black or white. No person is completely good or bad, successful, or dumb. No events, situation, or person can ever be entirely or wholly bad or good, right or wrong.

There are **two sides to everything**. Two sides to every issue, action, event, situation and person. Similarly, there are **two sides to arguments also**. There is nothing like the right argument or the wrong one. There is just a winning argument and a losing one.

Think of any topic which you perceive that cannot be defended. Let's take the case of terrorism. Any average person would say that terrorism cannot be justified or defended or argued for. But, in reality, even a heinous crime like terrorism is vigorously defended by people and countries which perpetuate them. These people and countries call terrorists as ' freedom fighters' who are fighting for freedom and a divine cause and that they have the blessing of GOD.

This duality is a boon and a problem.

The boon is that everything is relative to one another, and nothing is rigid or one-sided or even absolute.

The problem is that when things are connected, then there are as many views as minds. Every human being has a perspective and every person thinks he or she is right.

Over 30 years, I have carefully studied and noted the various styles and techniques people use while arguing, more so because I am a **criminal side lawyer**.

This book is the result of my experience and understanding of human nature and how people use logic and language to gain success in life.

I hope every reader can benefit from this book and succeed in life while practicing my approach.

KINDLY NOTE

In this book, examples are given for the limited purpose of understanding the principle of the technique. Readers are requested not to get into the merits and demerits of the arguments presented and just understand how the technique was applied.

The reader may feel that in some examples, the argument has not been won. While it may be true, if one looks closely, the argument has not been lost either. Therefore, not losing an argument or improving your situation from a loss to one of equality with the opponent has also been considered as winning.

Technique 1: Repeat and Repeat and Repeat.

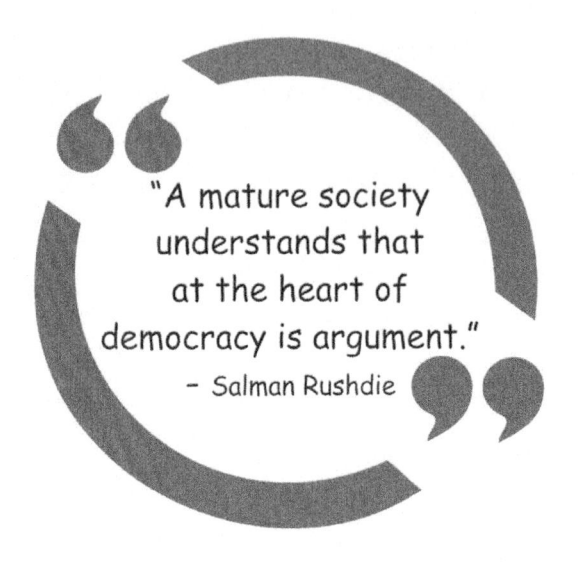

> "A mature society understands that at the heart of democracy is argument."
> – Salman Rushdie

Short **Description:**

In this technique, your opponent has **several strong points** to support his case while you have **only one**. You know that you will not be able to defend or counter any of the several points forwarded by your opponent. So, you should hold on tightly to your one strong point which you know the opponent cannot disagree with and keep **repeating it again** and again (maybe in different words), till the **opponent** gets exhausted with all his points and has nothing more or new to argue about. Exhaust the Opponent till he becomes silent.

Details Description :

Sometimes you may be in a situation in an argument/discussion, where the Opponent has several strong points on the topic of discussion. You may feel overwhelmed with the number of points and supporting data the Opponent may throw at you. You may feel cornered and choked as you may not have any defense/counter-arguments to counter your Opponent.

In such a situation, you must remember that whatever may be the topic of discussion, there **are always two sides to a coin.** There are always **two sides to every case** in discussion. There is no person, topic, situation which is completely good or completely bad or completely strong or completely weak. This is a universal law.

The point I am trying to make is that whatever may be the topic of discussion, there will be **AT LEAST ONE POINT** in your favor. You have to find **THAT ONE STRONG POINT IN YOUR FAVOR.** Keep repeating the same in different languages, words, phrases, and styles.

In such a situation, what happens is that your **opponent** will start very strongly with all his points but soon exhaust his entire big list of points. At the same time, you keep harping and emphasizing on that one vital point which your Opponent has no defense or rebuttal for. Very soon, he will be exhausted and run out of points and words while you will keep repeating that one argument and have the last word. Once your **opponent** has outrun all his points, he will either keep quiet(being tired from submitting his long list of points) or make the mistake of trying to counter or rebut your strong point, which is indefensible or rebuttable. In both scenarios, you will come out victorious and have the last words. You have to exhaust your **opponent** of his points till he has nothing more to say.

Example:

Situation: You and your friend are arguing about the viability of nuclear energy as the best source of power. Your friend has many points, and he is bombarding you with them. You are not well prepared. You just don't like nuclear power due to the possibility of a disaster and the consequences thereof.

Your friend says, "Nuclear power does not create pollution like other energy sources. Coal and other fossil fuels are the most significant sources of pollutants, which are causing global warming and taking mankind to the brink of destruction. Thus, it is undoubtedly the best option in the long run since it will not contribute to global warming."

You respond, "Hmm, but what about nuclear disasters?"

Your friend, "It is financially viable. The cost per unit is the lowest amongst all other energy sources."

You, "Nuclear accidents are inevitable. Who will be responsible for the death and destruction?"

Your friend, "There is enough nuclear fuel present on the earth to power humanity for eons to come, unlike other sources which are depleting so fast that many will not be available in a few decades."

You, "Nuclear disasters will leave millions dead. Who will take responsibility for these deaths?"

Your friend, "Nuclear energy is the future of our planet. Its benefits outweigh the disadvantages manifold."

You, "Yes, but nuclear energy will also cause the biggest disasters compared to other sources. How will mankind handle them? The disasters will ruin a place and make it inhabitable for centuries. Is mankind prepared for that?"

Your friend is quiet as he has no other new points!

Analysis :

What the reader has to see and understand in the above example is that your **opponent** has many points to support his contention. For whatever reason, you have only one strong point, and you are not prepared enough and even not informative enough to counter your **opponent's** points. So, you keep repeating your point in different ways till your opponent **exhausts all his points**.

Once your opponent runs through his point, he will either keep quiet or try to demolish your point, which cannot be demolished and will therefore fall into the trap of **countering an indefensible point**. In such a situation, there is a good chance that you will come out ahead even if you had fewer points and less preparation to argue the subject under discussion.

Words of Wisdom

"An argument is to find out who is right, and a discussion is to find out what is right"

-------Anonymous

Technique 2: Silence Speaks

> "Sometimes, silence is the best way to win an argument."
> – Jorge P. Guerrero

Short Description:

In this technique, you use silence as a tool to defend yourself. When you are in a not untenable position, he can use silence to counter the other. For any argument, a minimum of two people are required. In an argument of two, if one decides to remain silent, it is impossible for the other to continue.

Details Description:

Sometimes you are in a situation where you have **absolutely no defense** or answer or excuse against the other. Such situations can usually occur in close relationships or between the employer and employee. When you find yourself in such a situation where you have no defense, it is better to remain silent. This is because if you try to defend yourself since you don't have a strong case, you will be demolished instantly. As mentioned earlier, a minimum of two people is required for an argument. If one person decides not to participate, there is absolutely no way to continue the argument or to prevail over another.

In this technique keeping quiet is very important because the moment you try to explain your side of the story with excuses or weak points, you will land up, allowing the other side to come down heavily upon you with full guns blazing and completely destroy your weak submissions. **Therefore, silence is golden**. Silence is also a kind of communication. It is, in a way, saying something without saying anything. A **silent person can never lose an argument** because he simply does not participate in it.

It is also sometimes possible that because you choose to be silent, the other person in a fit of rage may use a loud tone and abusive or unparliamentary language. Such a scenario is even better because the other may feel guilty afterward for being rude and abusive to you, and there is a full possibility of getting a direct or indirect apology for the same even though it was you who was wrong. Thus, basically, the point I am trying to make is that there are many situations where it is more beneficial to remain quiet than getting into an argument.

Example:

Situation: Your wife asked you to run a few errands and get her a few things, including groceries for the party that night. You forgot. Now, there is no time to amend, and the party may be slightly spoilt due to your irresponsible and forgetful nature.

Your wife says in a cheerful voice, "Good Evening. Hurry up. Quickly give me all the groceries I had asked you to bring for tonight's party."

You, "Oops... Silent"

Wife, "What? Did you forget? Even after reminding you several times, you forgot? When will you become responsible? Why do you do this to me? When will you grow up and do something right for once? Now, what will happen to my dishes? Are you completely useless? You are "$#$#%@." (abuses)

You: Silent.
Analysis:

In the example above, you know that you are completely wrong and that you have no plausible excuse or defense. By remaining silent, you prevent the argument from moving forward and becoming even uglier. In the alternate, if you try to come up with some excuse, no matter how strong you may think it is, it will not work. **Remember, explanations, no matter how strong they are, they don't always work**. There are certain situations and certain people (parents or spouse), before whom the normal rules of logic and arguments don't work. This is due to the nature of the relationship you share with them. It is easier for a camel to pass through the eye of a needle than for you to win an argument against an angry wife. In the above example, if the same was against a friend, you may have employed another technique. But when you are facing a raging spouse, it's best to keep silent. Your wife will get angry. She will curse you. She will call you useless. She may even physically assault you. **But keep quiet**. Just keep quiet. There is a good chance that, despite all the disasters, the party may still turn out to be a success.

In such a case, there is a possibility that after 24-48 hours, your wife may realize her overreaction and bad behavior, and you may get a direct or an indirect apology for a situation in which you were wrong. Don't underestimate the power of silence. Don't feel that you always need to have the last word. Don't feel that if you don't speak, it means that you have lost the argument against your wife. **SILENCE IS MIRACULOUS. SILENCE SPEAKS**.

Words of Wisdom

"Silence is argument carried out by other means"
    ---Che Guevera

"A meaningful Silence is better than Meaningless words."
    ---Anonymous

"Never miss a good chance to shut up."
    ---Will Rogers

"I've begun to realize that you can listen to silence and learn from it. It has a quality and a dimension of its own".
    ----Chaim Potok

"Silence isn't empty; it is full of answers."
    ----Anonymous

Technique 3: Agree, Disagree

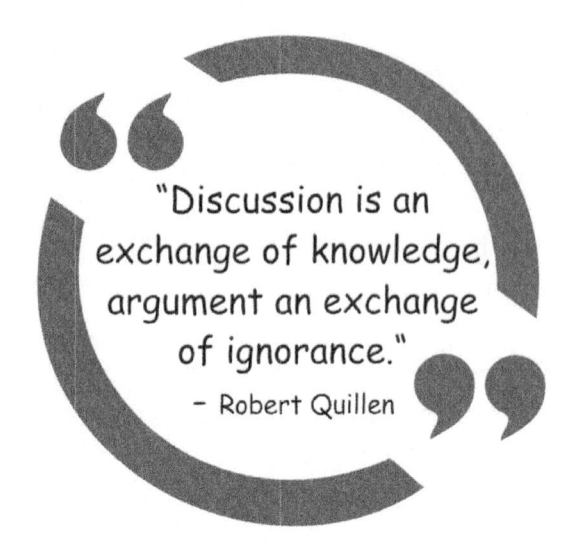

> "Discussion is an exchange of knowledge, argument an exchange of ignorance."
> – Robert Quillen

Short Description:

In this technique, even though you disagree with your **opponent,** due to respect, admiration, and reverence for the **opponent**, you politely first agree and then immediately disagree. This technique helps you in making your point without offending the other too much.

Details Description :

Many times you are in a situation where you are having an argument with someone you highly admire. This could be because of their age or relation to you or their profession—for example, parents, teachers, doctors, elder relatives…etc. Unfortunately, most of the time, people who are in a position of respect somehow feel that they are always right, due to their age, experience, and position of authority. Moreover, in many **cultures** and countries, especially in the east, having any disagreement with your parents, teacher, or elders is considered to be **impolite, rude, offensive or even ill-mannered.** So, the question arises about when you are having a genuine and persuasive disagreement with a respected person, then how should you go about it? If you treat that person badly through strong negative words, you are sure to upset him. If you are too light and courteous, you may never be able to convey your true and correct feeling and stand on the topic of discussion. How should you put your point across without being offensive? In such situations, the technique of agreeing and then disagreeing should be used. In this technique, when the elder or the respectable person makes a point which you do not agree with, then use positive words like **"I agree," "I understand," "I appreciate**," and then using a conjunction like '**BUT**' or a conjunctive adverb like '**HOWEVER**' you should politely disagree and forward your viewpoints. The phrase 'I Agree' is this case is not used in the context actually to agree with that person but is used to soften the impact of disagreement and to prevent hurting the ego of the elder or the respectable person.

One should refrain from using negative words and phrases like "I Don't Agree," "You are completely wrong," "Your statements don't make sense,"...etc.

As a thumb rule, please remember: **IT IS NOT WHAT YOU SAY BUT HOW YOU SAY IT.**

You could get away by saying the most horrendous and horrible things if you use a positive TONE and sugar coat your 'aggressive or contradictory points' with positive pre and post cursor words. You will be surprised by the number of arguments you will end up winning.

TRY IT!

Example:
Situation: You are having a discussion with your respected doctor on the topic of Allopathy vs. homeopathy/alternate pathy. You have great respect for your brilliant doctor, but there are some areas you completely disagree with him. Your doctor believes only in Allopathy while you also believe in homeopathy as well as other alternative therapies.

Doctor, "I say that Allopathy is the best way to treat humans as there is a strong science behind it. Homeopathy is a big scam. It is nothing but sugar pills. People recover only because of the placebo effect. There is no science behind homeopathy."

You, "**I agree with you, Sir; however,** there is immense data to show that millions of people have also benefited from homeopathy, Ayurveda, and naturopathy. I, myself, have used homeopathy several times and cured some diseases for which Allopathy has no answer. We cannot debunk other pathys. I am sure that every path has some usefulness in some specific areas of human health. Further, homeopathy is also based on science. Many people are not aware of it. Its practitioners believe that a substance that causes symptoms of a disease in healthy people would cure similar symptoms in sick people; this doctrine is called **similia similibus curentur, or "Like cures like."**

<u>Analysis:</u>

In the above example, you felt very compelled to disagree with his respectable doctor because you had an experience completely opposite to what the doctor was saying. You had two options. Either to use negative words and tell the doctor how uninformed and ignorant he is or use the: **Agree and then Disagree technique.** By using the phrase **"I Agree"** (Even though you don't agree), you were able to take the reins of the conversation into your hands in a positive way, and when you got the opportunity, you immediately used it to convey your point and message without being disrespectful or sounding rude. If in the alternate, if you have used "I disagree," the doctor would have not only felt a little upset but would not have given you a patient hearing. He could have also interrupted you in the midst of your submission to point out a fault in your information or looked at his watch and taken your leave. **If an argument is a war, then words are the weapons. Which weapon to use when deciding the fate of the war.**

Words of Wisdom

"You don't have to win every argument. Agree to disagree."
 ----Anonymous

"Agreement is made more precious by Disagreement."
 ----Publilius Syrus

"Honest disagreement is often a good sign of progress. "
 ----Mahatma Gandhi

"To disagree, one doesn't have to be Disagreeable."
 ----Barry Goldwater

"The fellow that agrees with everything you say is either a fool, or he is getting ready to skin you. "
 ----Kin Hubbard

Technique 4: Praise, Disagree

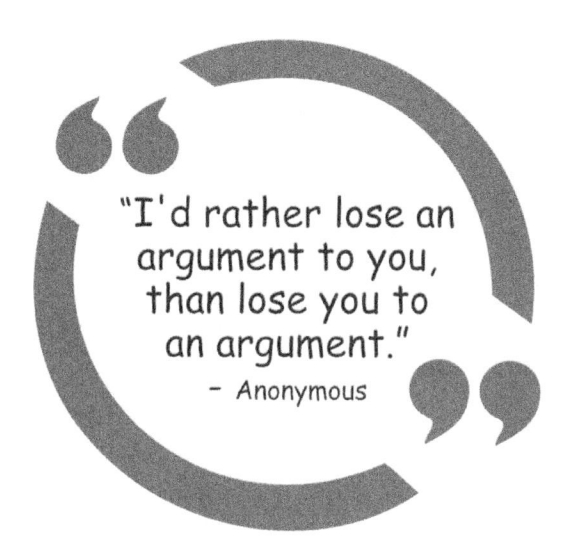

> "I'd rather lose an argument to you, than lose you to an argument."
> – Anonymous

Short Description:

Even though this technique may look a bit similar to the previous technique, it is, in fact, **one step ahead.** In this technique, even though you disagree with your **opponent**, due to your love and respect for him. So, you first praise him for satisfying his ego and for sounding polite then **immediately disagree.** This technique helps you to make your point **without offending** the other too much.

Details Description :

Sometimes, when you are in discussion with loved ones or people whom you consider very educated and intelligent, they surprise you by making the most **ridiculous, shocking, and bizarre arguments**. There are people you like, but sometimes even these people, whom you understand and whom you like to spend time with, make extremely inexplicable statements. In such situations, you want to counter their arguments with **love and respect rather than ridicule and aggression.** Using dissenting language towards anyone is very easy and is sure to make you unpopular and avoidable in social and public meetings. What is difficult is to maintain politeness in the face of a totally bizarre argument.

So, how to politely disagree with someone you like, respect, and care for is what this technique is all about.

The **'Art'** is to understand that all people like to be praised and to be spoken well about.

In this technique, you start your submission with words of praise for the other person, for example, **'You are so smart,' 'You are so intelligent,' 'You are educated,'**...etc. then immediately, you follow it up with a question, which asks the opponent whether your praise is valid or not and whether you praise is true and correct for him/her or not. For example, 'You are so intelligent, how can you say this? By using this technique, you first make the other **person feel good**, respected, and nice, and then suddenly, in the same flow, you make a **'U' turn** and show your disagreement by asking a question doubting whether the positive words of praise used by you still stand true and correct for that person. When you use nice words for the other person, **he/she is unable to continue their argument further** and defend your counter-argument. They feel that arguing further on that topic would make you change your mind about them from a positive view to a negative one.

Example:

Situation: You are having a conversation with your 13-year-old son. He is in the 8th grade, and for a reason best known to him, and out of the blue, he comes up with the assertion that he does not want to go to school anymore.

Son, "Papa, I don't like studying. I don't want to go to school."

You, "Son, you are highly intelligent, so bright, and so smart. Why would someone as smart as you be saying something like this? If you don't go to school, who will make the next spaceship?"

Analysis:

You **had two options** when hearing your son. Either you could have reacted negatively by saying, "Are you Crazy? Are you out of your mind? Who has put such stupid ideas in your mind?...etc.

But by using negative words, you would have made him defend himself and maybe even explain his statement. In such a situation, you should use reverse psychology. Your son is actually expecting you to be angry and to be mad at him. Your son knows that he is saying something which you won't like. So, instead of playing into his hands, you should use this technique of: **Praise and then disagree**. So, praise your son, even though he may not deserve it. Do it for putting your point across to him without challenging him. By calling your son smart and intelligent, you prevent him from continuing his argument as your son now feels that if he continues, then he will be seen as 'Not smart' or 'Not intelligent.'

Remember: Everybody likes to be praised. If in your praise, you mention what you feel about that person or expect out of that person or how you see that person, then you prevent him from acting or even behaving otherwise. People like to feel and be true to positive comments given by other people. If you call somebody well behaved, then that person will try to be well behaved just to be true to your positive statement.

Words of Wisdom

"When someone abuses me I can defend myself, but against praise I am defenseless".
---Sigmund Freud

"When you praise someone, you call yourself his equal".
-----Johann Wolfgang Von Goethe

"Praise makes good people better and bad people worse".
-----Anonymous

Technique 5: Faulty Presumptions

> "Behind every argument is someone's ignorance."
> – Louis D. Brandeis

Short Description:

In this technique, you identify the faulty presumption(s) or assumption(s) in your **opponent's** argument and point it out to him. All arguments have an underlying presumption. The conclusion of any argument is based on the presumptions in that argument. Consequently, the best way to break an argument is to break the presumption. **Demolish the presumption, Demolish the argument!**

Details Description :

Every statement we make has a presumption. Even a very common statement like "See you tomorrow" has a presumption that we are not going to die today and that we will be alive tomorrow. Therefore, if you want to weaken any person's argument, you should identify the presumptions in that person's argument and then weaken them. Presumptions are like the pillars of an argument. On top of these pillars you have your conclusion of your argument. If you break the pillars on which the argument sits, it comes down crashing.

Understanding presumptions:

Statement: - I am sure that Brazil will win the football match tomorrow.

A simple statement like this has the following presumptions

Presumption 1—That without any hurdle or problem, there will be a match tomorrow. You see, it is possible that it would rain. Or maybe a bomb blast or probably some other disaster because of which the match may be cancelled.

Presumption 2 –That the world will not end today. Even though this is highly impossible, still it is a presumption

Presumption 3—That the entire Brazilian team will be available tomorrow for the match. It is possible that a few players may not be available because they were delayed in transit coming from the previous match or due to ill health or due to an accident and so on and so forth. There are endless possibilities of the number of things that can go wrong before a match.

Therefore, as you see, whether probable or not, every statement has an underlying presumption(s). If you are able to identify the presumptions successfully, then you can break that argument on that point.

Now Let us carry forward the Brazil football match example ahead to analyze an argument and weaken it.

Example :

Situation: Your friend and you are discussing a football match where Brazil lost to France 1-3. Your friend is a Brazilian fan while you are a fan of the French team.

Your friend, "If Brazil had played player X instead of player Y then I am sure Brazil would have won."

You, "You are presuming that X would have played better than Y. Maybe, if X had been played, Brazil would have lost 1-5, who knows!"

Analysis:

In the above argument, your friend is presuming that player X **would have played better** than player Y. Nobody can ever say how X would have played because it never happened. So, the moment **you identify this presumption**, you can now weaken it and **break the argument**. Many people have a tendency, especially after an event has already taken place, to make presumptions with a positive or a better ending when there **is absolutely no basis** and reason for the same. It seems to stem from the human emotion of hope and desire. Many make the mistake of drawing positive conclusions if the circumstances had been different. They forget to note and take into account the other possibilities as their logical reasoning is marred with emotions attached to their inner desire for what they would have liked to see.

Words of Wisdom

"Some people find faults like there is a reward for it"

----Zig Ziglar

"Finding faults are good, it will make others aware of their mistakes but rectifying one's faults are best....many people can't do it".

-------Madhubanti Chakraborty

Technique 6: Statistics and Expert Opinion

> "The best way to win an argument is to begin by being right."
> — Jill Ruckelshaus

Short Description:

In this technique, you make use of **statistics and expert opinion** or research papers of **credible institutions** in your favor to support your submissions. Usually, people don't have counter arguments against statistics and expert opinion.

Details Description :

Sometimes you are arguing on a topic which has been **quantified and analyzed by statistics** or trustworthy research by credible institutions. In such cases, it is always better and desired to support your arguments with statistical data or expert opinion and research papers. If your **opponent** is ignorant about the statistics, he will immediately stop his argument as no one likes to **argue against credible data**.

Even if you don't remember the exact statistical data, but just the conclusion part of it, it is good enough for you to argue your case confidently. Most people don't get into the technicalities of any issue until and unless they are amongst research students and engineers. If your **opponent** is just a common Joe, throwing statistics will completely demolish his ability to argue his point further.

Example:
Situation: You and your friend are having a discussion about happiness and people from which country or regions seem to be the happiest. Your friend who is a supporter of America thinks that Americans are the happiest people on the planet while you think otherwise.

Your friend, "I am sure Americans are the happiest people in the world. After all, they have the maximum number of millionaires and billionaires. America is the most powerful and progressive country today and one of the biggest democracies. People have freedom of speech and the right to property and it is the land of dreams.

You, "Well, there was a study done by the Sustainable Development Solutions Network, powered by data from the Gallup World Poll and they have come up with a very interesting Happiness Index and a World happiness Report. According to this research and data, which is based on several parameters, Americans are not even in the top 10 list of most happy people. Americans come at a dismal 18, while the happiest people are from Finland, Denmark, and Switzerland. Surprisingly, their analysis also shows that there is no direct relationship between money and happiness. Many underdeveloped countries were happier than their developed counterparts. In fact Bhutan, a third world country is leading the way in giving importance to happiness and they have a full department in the government which focuses on the happiness of the people of their country.

Analysis:

In the above example, your friend gave his viewpoint based on his **personal perception and understanding** of happiness. Most people link two things as one causing the other, when in fact there is no cause-- effect relationship between them. Most people come to wrong conclusions by misunderstanding the cause----effect relationship. Your friend has come to the wrong conclusion that money (the cause) has resulted in happiness (effect).

Your argument is **based on research data** by a credible institute. Your submissions are based on statistics. Therefore, once you support your argument with research data or statistics, your opponent will have nothing to defend.

Words of Wisdom

"**There are three types of lies -- lies, damn lies, and statistics.**"
— Benjamin Disraeli

"*Facts are stubborn things, but statistics are pliable.*"
— Mark Twain

Technique 7: Two Wrongs ~~don't~~ Make a Right

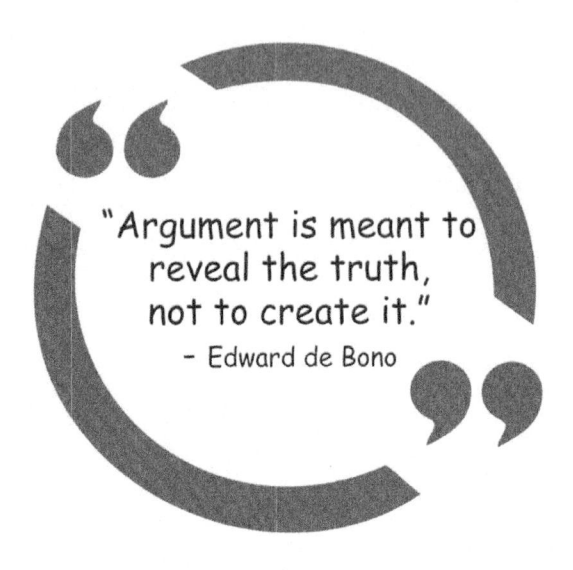

> "Argument is meant to reveal the truth, not to create it."
> – Edward de Bono

Short Description:

In this technique, you **reply to criticism with criticism**. You don't defend with a counter-argument because you have none. You are unable to defend an argument being forwarded by your opponent due to a mistake or a fault from your end. However, you are in the know-how of another situation (not the situation in discussion but some previous one) wherein your opponent had made a **similar mistake or blunder**. So, instead of countering and defending the present case (which you can't), you **divert** the argument to the

previous case where the **opponent** is unable to defend.

Details Description :

Sometimes you are at the receiving end of an argument because of some **blunder you have made**. In reality, you know that you have committed the blunder, and there is no strong defense for the same. If you try to defend it, you know you will make a total fool of yourself. This technique can be employed under those circumstances where your **opponent has also made previous blunders similar** to the one made by you. As mentioned earlier, as humans, we are not perfect, and we all have a past where we have done and committed acts of which we are not proud.

This technique can most effectively be used in **political discussions** where both parties (parties in discussion), over decades, have committed several similar blunders.

In politics, parties change, people change, but the blunders remain the same. A particular fault committed by one party when they were in power will be committed by the other party when they come to power. There is a constant stream of allegations and counter allegations between party members for acts and omissions done by their respective parties. In summary, all parties will have allegations of corruption, misuse of power, instigation of riots, unable to protect the national interest...etc.

So, if your **opponent** is having the **upper hand** in the discussion over a recent blunder committed by you or your party, you can divert the discussion to a similar blunder made by your opponent or his party. You counter criticism with criticism. Actually, your arguments should be limited to the recent event of blunder committed by you and its defense, if there is any. But since you don't have any defense, you **divert it to a previous blunder by your opponent**. If your **opponent** is not smart enough, he will fall prey to your diversionary tactics and start defending his blunder, which he may not be able to do successfully. The whole discussion will thus shift from the recent mistake, for which you lost the argument, to the previous blunder by your opponent for which you have the upper hand and may have the last word.

Frankly, two wrongs cannot make a right. You cannot justify your wrong action by citing a similar wrong action committed by your **opponent**. However, if he bites the bait, then you can successfully out-argue him.

Example:
Situation: You are the spokesperson for your party called 'A,' and your **opponent** (Z) is the spokesperson for his political party called 'B.' Recently, due to the illegal acts of some of your

party men, there were religious riots wherein 500 people died. Your **opponent** is attacking you and your party ferociously for the death of so many people. You are part of the ruling party.

Your **opponent** (on behalf of his party), "And, therefore, I say that the prime minister should immediately resign. It is under his tenure and leadership that such a heinous crime has been committed, and it is his party members who are responsible for instigating the crowd and causing riots, which resulted in the death of over 500 people."

You, "But Mr. Z(your Opponent), what about the riots in 1990, which were instigated by your party members. In those riots, over 1200 people had died. To date, your party has not taken responsibility for that. I say that, first, let your party acknowledge that they were behind those riots. Let your party give an apology to the nation for their heinous act."

Analysis:

In the above example, your opponent had the upper hand in the argument which you could not possibly defend. So, you **diverted the argument to a similar situation of blunder** against your opponent. This kind of diversion is wrong. You should argue only with regards to the topic being discussed. However, when cornered, you can use this technique effectively to get the upper hand.

Please note: The aim of the book is to give you both sides of the coin. Therefore, once you understand the principle of diversion, you can use it whichever way you want, depending on which side you are on. If you are on the winning side, you can identify the diversion and prevent the other from diverting, and if you are on the losing side, you can divert the topic to another where you have the advantage.

Words of Wisdom

"The moment we want to believe something, we suddenly see all the arguments for it and become blind to the arguments against it."
----George Bernard Shaw

"Use soft words and hard Arguments."
---Proverb

"I hate how after an argument I think of more clever things I should have said"
----Anonymous

Technique 8: Disclaimer

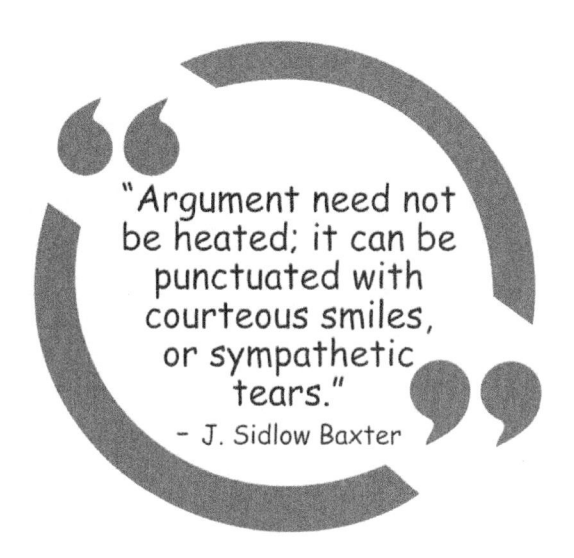

> "Argument need not be heated; it can be punctuated with courteous smiles, or sympathetic tears."
> – J. Sidlow Baxter

Short Description :

In this technique, you make a disclaimer by using **polite words** before you say something rude—**you sugar coat**. You sugar coat your potassium cyanide pill. It is based on the principle 'It is not what you say, but how you say it' Sometimes you can say the rudest, most scandalous things to your **opponent** and **get away with it** if it is said in a polite and sugar-coated manner with a nice tone.

Details Description :

There are hundreds and thousands of fake and evil people floating amongst us. This creates a situation where sometimes you need to **say rude things to these phony people.** You need to be rude not because you like being rude but because somebody needs to show these people a mirror and tell them who they truly are. Somebody needs to expose these people's lies. To do this, one has to be a little tactful. Directly confronting these evil people may **harm us**, so, therefore, one can use the technique mentioned above to expose them as well as to convey your disgust to them without sounding too aggressive and hostile.

A disclaimer is a **statement which a person makes so as to not take responsibility for his statements.** Disclaimers are words and phrases which give us **a soft landing** to our rude comments. Disclaimers can help you in saying the meanest and rudest things without sounding bad or without spoiling the relationship and without offending the other.

This technique can be successfully used where you want to make personal remarks about a person. Some examples of disclaimers are:

1. Please don't misunderstand me, but...

2. I don't want to offend you, but....

3. With all due respect, but.....

4. I don't mean to be rude, but.....

5. I admire your hard work, but....

Example:
Situation: A politician who is standing for elections from your area is on an election campaign. He has a very bad antecedent, having been an accused in a murder case and has several criminal cases pending against him. Unfortunately, it is candidates like these who stand and win elections on the basis of creating fear, money, and misuse of power. So, your area politician has just given his election speech citing reasons of why you should vote for him. You want to confront him or just argue against him with regards to his criminal antecedent and show him a mirror without taking him on directly.

Politician (After finishing his election speech for votes), "And therefore, my brothers, sisters, and countrymen. For the several reasons stated by me in my speech, I, therefore, conclude to say that I believe myself to be the best candidate for the upcoming election."

You, "Sir, with all due respect and without meaning to offend you, aren't you facing criminal charges in 4 cases?"

Politician, "Those are all politically motivated fake cases."

You, "Sir, I don't mean to be rude but isn't your son married to the daughter of Mr. X, who is a well-known builder and a drug supplier."

Politician, "Those are just rumors to tarnish my image and reputation."

You, "Sir, I truly admire your speech but hasn't your first wife filed a domestic violence case against you?"

Analysis:

In the above example, you are exposing and arguing against the politician indirectly by using **disclaimer statements** as precursors. The disclaimer phrases are cushioning you against your rude but true facts. You have conveyed to the politician and to the several people indirectly that you will not be voting for him, and at the same time, you have made people aware (assuming some people did not know) why you intend not to vote for him. To the untrained eye, the above case may not look and feel like an argument. Yet, it is. It is a disagreement. The politician wants you to vote for him while you want to do otherwise.

Words of Wisdom

"Raise your words, not your voice. It is rain that grows flowers, not thunder.
 ---RUMI

"Every friendship needs one argument just to see how stable it really is
 --Anonymous

Technique 9: Apples VS Oranges

> "Anger is never without an argument, but seldom with a good one."
> – Indira Gandhi

Short Description:

In this technique, your **opponent**, unable to counter your arguments, **diverts** the discussion to an **entirely new topic**, which is **totally unrelated** to the topic of discussion at hand because he has a better advantage to discuss the diverted topic.

Details Description:

Whenever you are going to be in a position of strength in an argument, your opponent is going to employ all the tricks up his sleeve to divert the topic. Your **opponent** will open up an **entirely new front**, new topic of discussion, which is totally unrelated to the topic of discussion at hand. This is a **diversion technique** used by your **adversary** to change the topic of discussion to a topic that is favorable to him. You should be alerted, not fall into the trap of this diversion and continue to bring your **adversary** back to the real and main topic of discussion. You should keep control of the flow of discussion in every argument. If you don't, **he** will try **to slip away to another topic** as it suits him more. Please, note that in every conversation, one person always has the control of the flow of conversation in that discussion. **THAT PERSON SHOULD BE YOU.**

This technique may seem similar to technique no 7, but there is a big difference between the two techniques. In technique 7, the diversion was to a similar topic which had happened in the past, but in this technique, your **opponent** opens up a completely new and unrelated topic.

Example:

Situation: You and some office colleagues are discussing the beauty of technology and the splendor of living in present times in the digital age, with computers, the internet, and Google. One of your colleagues has a habit of always contradicting you.

You, "I feel lucky to be alive in this present day and age. It's so exciting. Computers, internet, Google, Artificial Intelligence...etc. Every few years, man can do things which were at one time only dreams, which were at one time thought to be impossible and were subjects left for sci-fi films. **I love technology.**"

Opponent colleague, "But what about animals? Every year, more and more species are disappearing. More and more animals are being killed. Animals are mistreated**. I hate technology.**"

You, "You are right about animals, but we are discussing technology and how wonderful it is. I think you missed the main topic of our discussion. Anyways..."

Analysis:

Read the above example carefully. The opponent colleague is **interested only in countering you**. There are some people who, whatever you say, they will say the opposite. Their aim is to oppose you. Period. Their aim is not to give logical reasons and opinions for their submissions. For opposing, they will give **such illogical arguments** as well as reasons and conclusions that it will surprise you; it may even be **so bizarre** that it will take some time for you to comprehend what they are saying altogether. For some, the response of the opposing colleague may seem related to the topic of the discussion, BUT on closer inspection, you will realize that it is **irrelevant**. Even if the opponent's arguments are true and correct when it comes to animals, they are unrelated to the main topic of the technology discussion.

The discussion had absolutely nothing to do with animals or thereabouts. But your opponent changed it to animals, bad treatment and further went on to conclude something completely unrelated to his premise but was in contrast and contradiction to your assertion. One has to be very **careful against such people** because you may not have the art of talking illogical, but they have it.

Actually, the right response of the colleague should have been with regard to technology. Maybe he could have given reasons for the ills of technology. However, he has completely gone tangential. Like I said earlier, he was not interested in discussing technology. He was only interested in opposing you. Since he could not oppose you by countering your strong points, he created a new topic and opposed that and somehow linked it with your topic even though there was no link.

In such situations, it is important to be aware and alert because people hardly listen to what is being said and discussed. They have their own agenda. Their own biased views. Somehow people are able to bring in **their biases in every conversation**, even if they are not related. They live in their own world and keep talking about topics interesting to them only. In the above discussion, the opponent has completely changed the topic to something else. If at this stage, a third colleague who is present, picks up the animal topic, you will be surprised to see how the subject will totally change from a discussion about technology to animals. If that happens, you will realize that somehow your **adversary's** assertion seems to have prevailed over yours. Thus, you must immediately **point out** to him that the topic of discussion was something else and had no bearing to animals and therefore, your conclusion that you love technology still holds and cannot be compared to the reason why the Opponent hates technology

YOU ARE TALKING APPLES AND HE IS TALKING ORANGES.

Words of Wisdom

"A relationship with no arguments is a relationship with a lot of secrets."

"Say what you mean, but don't say it mean.
----Andrew Wachter

Technique 10: Ad-hominem Attack

> "When you have no basis for an argument, abuse the plaintiff."
> – Marcus Tullius Cicero

Short Description:

In this technique, your **opponent verbally attacks you** instead of the topic in discussion. This usually happens when your **adversary** is cornered, he has no escape from your strong arguments, and he is unable to find any strong counter-argument. So, in frustration as well as irritation, and **to divert the debate or the discussion**, he starts to attack you fiercely at the same time personally.

Details Description:

Many times you will be in a debate where you are winning hands down. You are completely demolishing all the arguments of your Opponent, and he has no escape route or counter defense. In such situations, he may try to create a diversion by attacking you personally rather than the topic in the discussion so as to shake you, unsettle you, and divert the topic to something in which you may not have much defense.

You should be **very alert**, not to fall into the **trap of your Opponent**. If you start defending your personal attacks, then the topic will change from the real topic of discussion, which you were winning, to the allegations against you in the personal attack. If you start defending the personal attack, you will fall prey to exactly what your **adversary** wanted to do to escape the real topic of discussion. So you have to be alert to **identify the opponent's strategy**, instead of countering the personal attack, you have to show your **adversary** that you are not unsettled or perturbed, and you have to keep getting him back to the real topic. You must, in plain words, tell **him** that his answers and **submissions should be limited to the real topic** of discussion and nothing else or outside that.

It is quite easy to get swayed into countering the personal allegations against you because it is human and a natural instinctive response to start defending oneself. So, you should be very aware and sharp and alert and keep bringing your Opponent **back to the real topic** of discussion.

Example:

Situation:
You are a social activist. You believe in organic food and a cleaner environment.

You are in a debate where you are advocating the ban of pesticides as they are extremely harmful in the long run. However, you have a checkered past, where on one occasion, a girl in your office had made allegations against you as a part of the 'ME TOO' movement. You were given a clean chit. But the stain still remains.

You, "And so, as I said in my presentations, for the several reasons that I have cited, I can say confidently that the use of pesticides is more harmful than not, in the long run for mankind. I propose a complete ban on all pesticides, and I propose the growth of organic food."

Your Opponent (Unable to defend your strong and convincing points), "I think first we should ban you. It was horrible, what you did to that poor helpless girl. A person like you, who has no ethics and morals, is trying to teach the world what is good and bad. How can you even have the guts to think that you can teach the world when you need to be taught a good lesson for doing what you did.

You, "Mr abc (your **opponent**), the topic of discussion and debate is 'The use and misuse of pesticides in farming,' I would appreciate that you do not divert from this topic and keep your submissions limited to the same.

Analysis:

In the above example, what is important for you to understand is how skillfully, by **borrowing your own word 'Ban',** the opponent has diverted the topic of discussion from a discussion on 'The use and misuse of pesticides' to 'personal allegations against you for something from your past.' The strategy **he** is trying to play is by **showing you in poor light,** he is trying to convince others that even your **ideas and views are poor**. Now, even though there is absolutely no connection between your ideas and your previous act; your opponent is trying to link both to bias the minds of others.

In such a situation, if you start to defend yourself that the allegations against you were wrong and that you have been given a clean chit…etc. You will **fall prey** to your opponent's trick as the discussion will shift to that topic. So, you have to politely bring him back to your topic of discussion.

Words of Wisdom

"Ad hominem is a notoriously weak logical argument. And is usually used to distract the focus of a discussion - to move it from an indefensible point and to attack the Opponent."
         ---- *Lord Aquitainus Attis* ~
Furies of Calderon by Jim Butcher."

" I always think it's a sign of victory when they move on to the ad Hominem."
         ---Christopher Hitchens

"That's not an ad Hominem, you idiot!"

Technique 11: Anger, Anger, Go away!

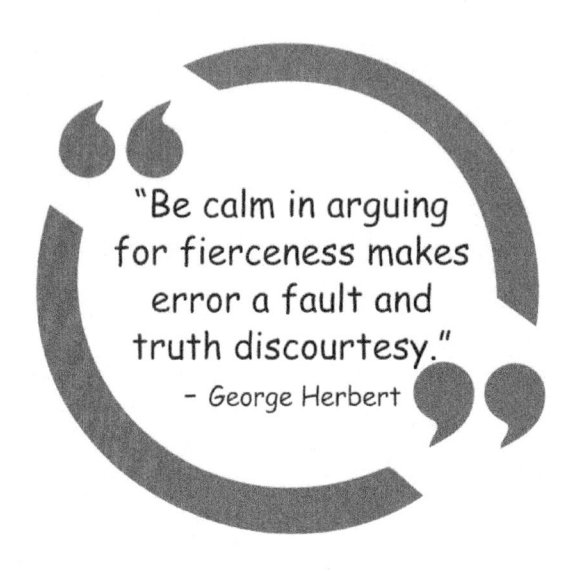

> "Be calm in arguing for fierceness makes error a fault and truth discourtesy."
> – George Herbert

Short Description:

In this technique, you use your **ability to be calm**, relaxed, and composed during an argument and **not lose your temper**. If your **opponent** is loud, aggressive, and abusive, even though he may be 100 % right about his argument, he may still lose it if you counter his aggression with **serenity and grace**. So basically, you don't counter his argument, which maybe you can't. **You counter his aggression.**

Details Description:

There are many occasions when you are arguing **against a loud**, aggressive, and abusive person. These people are very sensitive and **lose their temper at the drop of a hat.** They take things personally and treat every conversation as a war where they want to have the last word. These people argue as if it's a matter of life and death. They have no patience to hear other people or to accept the viewpoint of others. As soon as these people are challenged, **they become very violent and abusive.**

While arguing, never lose your temper. If you lose your temper, you will lose the argument, no matter how well-founded your argument is.

This technique can be put into action against those people who are loud, aggressive, and abusive. There are some people who convert every small discussion into a debate or an argument. And they always need to have the last word and win the argument. It is effortless to instigate such people and bring them into a state of anger.

In such a situation, you should use the opponents **'Anger problem'** in your favor. Don't lose your temper under any circumstances. Let the opponent flair up. If possible, add oil to his fire. **Anger is a temporary madness.** When anger envelops your **opponent**, he is **bound to make mistakes**, say illogical and unreasonable things and even attack you verbally.

That's IT. Once a person loses it, you have won. It doesn't matter how right your opponent's arguments are. It doesn't matter how weak your arguments are. **Loss of temper = loss of argument** (at least in the eyes of all the people present at that moment). This is a very effective tool to use in group debates and discussions of sensitive issues. Always study your opponent for weakness in his preparation or **weakness in his personality**.

Remember, as a thumbs rule that: A person who keeps calm and doesn't lose his temper always wins an argument even if he is wrong.

<u>**Example:**</u>
<u>**Situation:**</u> Loud arguments and personal attacks are common in extended family meets. One can be sure that in a large extended family, some cousins will **hate each other.** You and your Cousin (both of you can't see each other eye to eye) are sitting in a large extended family meeting group. Both of you are arguing on a point of disagreement. You are aware that your cousin has **an 'Anger Problem'**. In contrast, you have control over your emotions.

Your Cousin (After he loses his temper), "What do you mean? Am I wrong? How can you say that I don't understand anything? What do you think of yourself? I am more educated than you. I am not stupid. You are fu** stupid and ignorant. You are outrightly, Dumb."

You (in a cool and relaxed tone), "Relax, my dear brother. I am only saying that your point of view is not acceptable. Don't be angry."

Your Cousin (in a loud and agitated voice), "I am not angry. Who says I am not relaxed. I am utterly relaxed. You are not relaxed. I am fine. But you are an idiot who thinks no end of himself. You believe that you are right, and the others are wrong."

You, "May I get you a glass of water? Please relax. Your blood pressure will shoot up."

Analysis:

In the above example, irrespective of the topic of discussion between you and your cousin, you will be successful in your argument in the **eyes of the rest of the people present at that moment**. Instead of replying to anger with anger, you should **reply to anger with calmness** and composure. You should speak softly and with respect. The wise men have said that **'Anger is temporary madness'** and therefore, the moment your **opponent** loses his temper, know it for sure that you **have won**. All you have to do then is not to get pulled in the anger regardless of the language and insults your opponent may bestow upon you. Remember, never take any argument personally. Be a little detached. In such a situation, no matter how good and correct your cousin may be, because of his anger, you will win your case, at least in the eyes of other people, despite the weakness of your record.

Words of Wisdom

"Try to manage your anger since people can't manage their stupidity."

"Speak when you are angry, and you will make the best speech you will ever regret."
---Ambrose Bierce

"If you are patient in one moment of anger, you will escape a hundred days of sorrow."
—Chinese proverb

"If you hate a person, then you're defeated by them."
---Confucius

"For every minute you are angry, you lose 60 seconds of happiness."

Technique 12: Proverb

> "Never argue when you're winning."
> – Laurell K. Hamilton

Short Description:

A proverb is a short well-known saying containing a **wise thought**, a general truth, or piece of advice. In this technique, you counter your **opponent**'s argument with a proverb rather than a defensive counter-argument. **The proverb itself is the counter-argument.**

Details Description :

There are proverbs for every situation of life. Proverbs **summarize the wisdom of mankind**, which it has acquired through ages. However, there is a catch. For every proverb, there is also an equal and opposite proverb. So, there are proverbs for

both sides of the argument. There are proverbs for "For" and "For against" a particular situation or topic. As an example, please find below a list of proverbs and their opposite proverbs.

There are situations when what you want to say can be summarized **aptly through a proverb**. If your thoughts can be effectively conveyed through a proverb, then you must use them as people usually don't challenge or argue against proverbs as everybody believes that proverbs capture the quintessential wisdom of mankind and arguing against them would make them seem foolish.

People can argue and find mistakes against another person's views points, but they cannot argue against the timeless wisdom of a proverb.

PROVERB	OPPOSITE PROVERB
All good things come to those who wait	But time and tide wait for no man
The pen is mightier than the sword	But Actions speak louder than words
Wise men think alike	Fools seldom differ

The best things in life are free	There's no such thing as a free lunch
Birds of a feather flock together	Opposites attract
You're never too old to learn	You can't teach an old dog new tricks
Absence makes the heart grow fonder	Out of sight, out of mind
Too many cooks spoil the broth	Two minds are better than one

Example:
Situation:
You are a teacher. You teach the 9th Grade. The average age of the class is 14 years. You are appalled to notice that more than 50 percent of the class is overweight. You decide to take up the matter.

You, "Students, I see that most of you are overweight. Why are you people over eating?"

Student 1, "No teacher, we are not over eating. We are growing children; we need food for better growth."

You, "Yes, you need food, but only up to a certain amount and calorie. Over that amount, you will develop health problems."

Student 2, "We feel hungry. The hunger clearly indicates that our body is asking for food. Last time, you only told us that we must listen to our bodies."

You, "Yes, but, you must know the difference between real hunger and cravings."

Student 3, "When I am hungry, I can't concentrate."

You, "Students. I understand your points and arguments BUT, please understand, **WE EAT TO LIVE AND NOT LIVE TO EAT.**"

Students: Quite

Analysis:

In the above example, you have conveyed your thoughts by a **small and effective proverb**. If you had not taken the help of the proverb, maybe you would have landed up arguing more and more with the students. The students are also making rational points but the moment they hear a well-known proverb, they understand that the **proverb is backed with wisdom** and that they should listen and understand that wisdom rather than continue the argument.

Proverbs are a very effective way of getting your message across to people without getting embroiled in a **never ending argument.**

Words of Wisdom

"My anger, hate, arguments, and fight are expressions. These show how I feel at different times, but they don't affect my love and respect for you. You need to understand this."
-------Kirti Chowdhary

"Arguments are healthy. They clear the air."
----Anonymous

Technique 13: Loaded words

> "If you go in for argument, take care of your temper. Your logic, if you have any, will take care of itself."
> – Joseph Farrell

Short Description :

A loaded word or phrase is something that has strong **positive or negative connotations** beyond its ordinary definition with the potential to generate strong emotions. In this technique, you **mask your argument with a loaded word** so that you further your argument or **divert the main argument** on the bias created by your loaded word rather than the merit of the argument.

Details Description:

Sometimes you are in a discussion where the subject, person or thing in question is such that it has **two completely different aspects.**

Sometimes you are in a discussion where the topic, person, or thing in question is such that it has two completely different aspects. **One very positive and the other extremely negative.** Your Opponent is arguing for one of the aspects, and you divert the topic to the other aspect to counter his argument. You do this because there is no way you can counter the aspect being agitated by your **adversary.** Thus, you mask your argument with a loaded word to skew the conversation and skillfully divert the subject to the other side, which your opponent cannot successfully argue. You use **strong, loaded words to influence the minds of other people,** so that the word you used prevents the other person from continuing their argument or traps them in an argument that the other person is doomed to lose. By using loaded words, you unilaterally bias an unfounded argument and divert the discussion so that your loaded word becomes the diversion and the subject of the argument instead of the subject initiated by the opponent

Examples of some **positively loaded words** -- darling, angel, intelligent, beautiful, genius.

Examples of some **negatively loaded words** -- molester, stalker, cheat, psycho, crazy.

Examples where a positive loaded word is used

Situation, "Your friend and you are having a discussion on the new documentary called 'Wild Wild Country' on Netflix, made on the life of spiritual guru OSHO. Your friend knows that you are a follower of Osho, and he purposely brings up this topic to hurt you."

Your friend, "Have you seen that documentary, Wild Wild Country on OSHO? My God, what a pervert he was. What a fake."

You, "Who Osho? The enlightened master Osho? The greatest spiritual master of the 20thcentury."

Your friend, "That's all, bullSh**. He was not enlightened."

Analysis:

In the above example, you have used a positive loaded word like ' **enlightened master**' '**greatest**' to divert the whole conversation. Your friend wanted you to defend his allegation of Osho being a pervert, but by using the loaded word, your friend landed up **trying to defend your positive loaded** word 'enlightened master.' You changed the whole direction of the argument by 180 degrees using the loaded word.

Another example of using a positive loaded word but in a slightly different way.

Situation: It's Saturday night, and you are going out with your friends to watch a football game and then for a few drinks at a friend's place. You will be leaving your wife alone at home. You know that your wife will not like this. Plus, she is a control freak. She likes to control every aspect of your life. You are getting dressed up to go but suddenly she notices this.

Your Wife, "Hey, Where are you going, ?"

You, "Hi, Angel, my beautiful darling wife. Just going out with friends to watch football."

Your Wife, (after a little pause), "Okay, go, but come back soon."

Analysis:

You have successfully used loaded words like 'angel,' 'beautiful,' 'darling' to **influence the mind of your wife.** When you use good words for a person, it is extremely difficult for that person to **behave in contrast** to those words. In this case, you used the word 'Angel.' So, it becomes very difficult for her to behave otherwise. If you had not used these loaded words, she may have come down heavily upon you. She would have cribbed that you are leaving her alone and that you should have told her earlier...etc. but by calling her darling and angel, you have psychologically manipulated her to behave like one. Unknowingly, her mind feels good that you feel she is an angel, and she doesn't want you to change your opinion about her. Her mind quickly calculates all the permutations and combinations, and then she asks you to come back home early. Note, your wife still wants to have the last word and still wants control. But her control is now limited to the time of coming back, rather than not going for the game at all.

You had **actually won the argument even before it began.** Some readers may think that there was no argument at all. But, that's the beauty of this technique. You **thwarted an argument** even before it began. Please, keep in mind that you always knew that your wife would disagree with your program. By using weighted and charming words, you got your way. You won the impending disagreement.

An example where a negative loaded word is used.

Situation: You and your friend are discussing Woody Allen films. There is no doubt that Woody

Allen is a Genius. However, he has a dark side also. There were allegations of him molesting his adopted daughter, and also many people did not approve of him marrying his own adopted daughter. So, there are two very strong opposing sides to his personality. **One good and one bad.**

Your friend, "I love Woody Allen films. He is such a genius. His directing style is so amazing. He understands human nature so well. I just love him."

You, "Who Woody Allen? That molester?"

Your friend, "No, no, charges against him were not proved. He is not a molester."

Analysis :

In the above example, your friend is absolutely right about the genius of Woody Allen. But, you don't like him(whatever may be the reason). So, by using a loaded word like 'molester', you divert the whole conversation to discussing your loaded word. If you had not used that loaded word, the conversation would have continued with regards to his films and what a great director he is. However, with just a single strong loaded word, you diverted and shifted the whole argument and had your friend defending your word.

Words of Wisdom

"Rule #1 during arguments: if you're losing, start correcting their grammar."

"Some marriages depend on domestic arguments the way the courts depend on litigation ."
                          ---Mason Cooley

Technique 14: Emotional Versus Logical

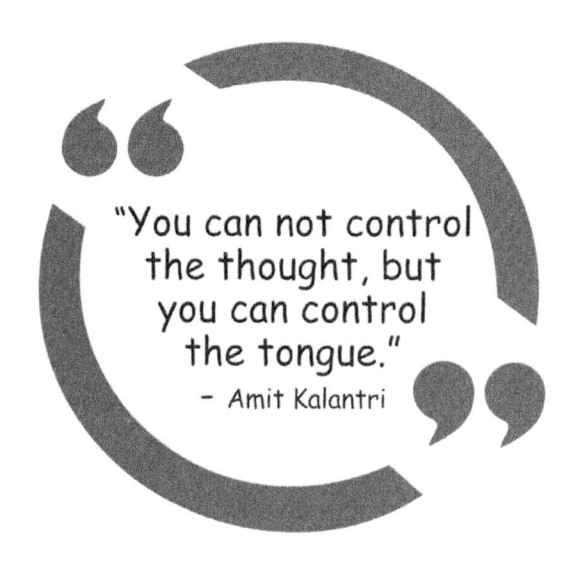

> "You can not control the thought, but you can control the tongue."
> – Amit Kalantri

Short description:

In this technique, when an opponent strikes you with strong logical reasoning to support their case, and you have none to counter, you can use **emotional arguments** to introduce bias in the arguments. **Humans are emotional creatures** and easily swayable with emotional arguments. In general, people understand emotional issues much better and faster than logical issues.

Details Description:

This technique can be used when you **don't have a counter defense to the logical** argument used by the other side, but you have some emotional points which you feel you can use to sway the argument in your favor. Humans don't always react with logic. Humans can easily be **swayed with an appeal to emotions. Heart,** somehow always seems to win over the **Head** in the case of arguments. Human beings are not just flesh and blood; they are a bundle of feelings and emotions. Even the most logical person can be influenced if you know how to make him emotional.

Example:

Situation: You are a lawyer. Your client (Mrs. ABC) is a lady who is 70 years old. She is accused of having committed forgery. You are arguing for her bail before a judge, and you are aware of her underlying poor health. You use the health issue to your advantage by appealing to the emotions of the Judge.

Your opponent lawyer, "My lord, prima facie, it is clear that Mrs. ABC was involved in this crime, and the police have also registered the First Information Report only after they were themselves convinced of her complicity. So, I say that Mrs. ABC should not be granted bail as she may tamper with evidence and influence witnesses."

You, "My lord, kindly appreciate that Mrs. ABC is a senior citizen. She also has cancer. She was operated on last year. She needs constant medication, and she is also financially very weak. She is a widow and has no support."

Judge, "ok, I will grant her bail on several conditions. She should not leave the city without permission or contact any witness."

Analysis :

In the above example, you have not countered your opponent's argument with logical arguments but have gone on emotional ones. Frankly, a court has to decide on the **merits of the case** and not on emotions. But here, you have successfully used her old age and sickness to **sway the emotions of the judge** in your favor. Please, bear in mind, no matter how much any human being may try to be neutral and not biased, but **the reality is that all humans suffer from some bias** or the other. If you are **able to appeal to the emotion** of any human being, you can influence that person in your favor.

Words of Wisdom

"All logical arguments can be defeated by the simple refusal to reason logically."
             ---Steven Weinberg

"Never argue with a liar. You can't win because they believe their own lies."
                     ---Anonymous

Technique 15: Condition First

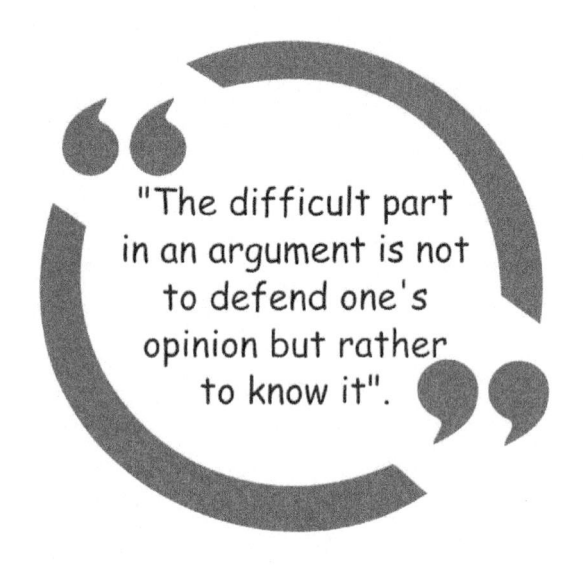

> "The difficult part in an argument is not to defend one's opinion but rather to know it".

Short Description:

In this technique, you put a **'condition pre-requisite'** before moving ahead in the argument. If you have a powerful point which the **opponent** cannot defend, you can **use that point as a 'condition pre-requisite'** to proceed further in the argument. Since your condition is not defendable by the **opponent**, there are high chances of him **backing off** from the argument. Otherwise, he will try to argue a losing argument on your condition pre-requisite point.

Details Description:

There are situations where both **parties have equally strong points** and both are arguing vehemently and successfully. In such situations, if you want to win the argument, you can use this technique where you can introduce a 'condition pre-requisite' in the conversation before continuing the argument. You tell your opponent that **'First', your point needs to be argued and settled and then only the other points should be considered.**

By introducing this condition of **my point 'First', you take control of the flow of the argument.** The other party is forced by you to defend your condition requisite and more often than not they will not succeed. In contrast, also be aware that your **opponent** uses this technique against you. If he does, you have to get your **opponent** back to the main argument and ignore the condition requisite.

Example:
Situation: Your friend and you are arguing about who was the best American president during recent times. Your friend is a big supporter of Bill Clinton. He just can't stop praising Mr. Clinton, his policies, and everything he did for America. However, you think otherwise.

Your friend: Bill Clinton's foreign policy was the best ever.

You: But let's **first** talk about his policy on Monica Lewinsky?

Your friend: It was during Bill's time that America had the lowest unemployment rate.
You: Let's **first** talk about why he lied on oath and misguided the whole nation.
Can a liar ever be a good President?

Your friend: He took America to new heights with financial changes he brought to the financial system of our country.

You: Let's **first** discuss what changes he brought to the Oval office and how he misused his authority and power against an intern. Let's first talk about these issues. For me, the character of a person is everything. Let's discuss first why he cheated on his wife.

Your friend: Well, Monica Lewinsky was an isolated mistake that he made....blah blah blah........(your friend bites the bait and starts to discuss your condition pre-requisite question which he will fail to defend ultimately.) You have successfully got your friend down to discussing your strong point in the argument.

Analysis: In the above-mentioned example, your aim was to put a **condition pre-requisite (My point first)** in the argument of a point that was in your favor. There is no way your **opponent** can justify the Monica Lewinsky debacle of Bill Clinton. So, you kept talking about it and kept putting it as a condition requisite before moving ahead in the discussion. Your opponent tried to ignore your 'condition requisite' a few times, but seeing you adamant, he lost patience and bit the bait of discussing your strong point. Once your **opponent** does this, jump on him and demolish his weak arguments against your strong point.

Again, it's a matter of who is controlling the flow of the arguments. Always, the person who controls the flow wins the argument. Here, you have taken control of the flow of the argument by introducing the prerequisite condition and getting your opponent to follow your requisite.

Words of Wisdom

"**Learning humility is a prerequisite for grace**"
                         ---- **Philip Yancey**

"**It's bad enough that your happiness is conditional upon your own behavior. When you start making it conditional upon other people's behavior, you are in serious trouble.**"
                 ---**Anonymous**

Technique 16: Seek and you shall find- Faulty logic

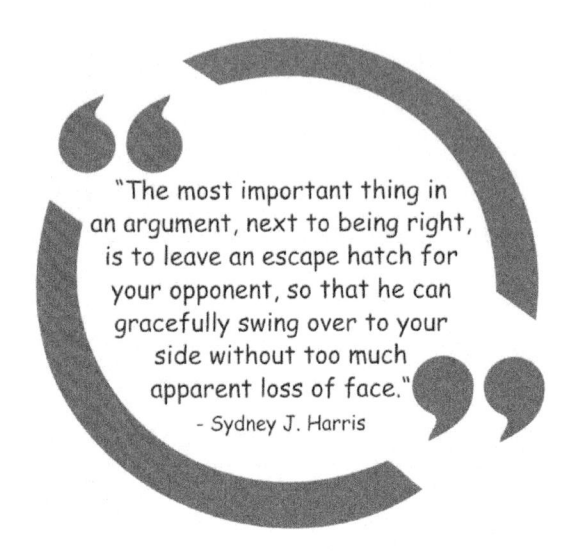

> "The most important thing in an argument, next to being right, is to leave an escape hatch for your opponent, so that he can gracefully swing over to your side without too much apparent loss of face."
> - Sydney J. Harris

Short Description:

In this technique, you find a fault in the logical reasoning of the **opponent**'s argument. Once you point out the **flaw in the argument**, the **opponent** will be left silent. However, before you find fault, you must update yourself on the various kinds of faults that usually people make. They are known as fallacies. A **list of the most common fallacies is given below**. The reader may study them further in detail as per requirement. It is

beyond the scope of this book to discuss all the fallacies in detail.

Details Description:

Logic is not easy for people to understand. Nearly all people, at some time or another, make illogical statements. Human beings are very complex. Many factors influence their thoughts and views. Humans may speak out of emotions, hopes, desires, etc., and none of their statements may be logical. Thus, it is first very important to understand what are the different fallacies in logic and then use them to identify them in the argument of your **opponent**. **Spot the fallacy, win the argument.** There are several types of fallacies. Few popular fallacies are discussed below:

The Fallacy of Hasty generalization :

In this kind of fallacy, you make a **significant conclusion** based on a minimal/inadequate **sample data size**. You generalize based on a tiny sample and wrong interpretation of that small sample. Example: 'I went to London. I met 5 people. All five people had a Vodafone mobile connection. Everyone in London uses Vodafone mobile networks only'. The conclusion could be wrong because maybe this person was visiting a

Vodafone store or a community that had a special scheme from Vodafone.

The Fallacy of Red Herring: In this type of logical fallacy, an **irrelevant issue** is raised to divert attention from the main argument.

For example: In a debate while arguing whether God exists, someone might argue that believing in God gives peace of mind. This would be an example of a red herring since whether religion can have a positive effect on people is irrelevant to the question of the existence of God.

The Fallacy of slippery slope: In this type of logical fallacy, a person illogically argues that if one particular thing has to be accepted, then he will have to accept another closely related thing also, which in turn will make him accept still another thing. Accordingly, this will lead to the conclusion that the **opponent** is committed to something absurd or unacceptable.

Example: "The government should not prohibit drugs. Otherwise, it should also ban alcohol or cigarettes, and then fatty food and junk food must be regulated too. The next thing you know, the government would force us to brush our teeth and do exercise everyday".

The Fallacy of Begging the question (circular argument): In this type of logical fallacy, when a person is arguing a particular claim/point, the claim/point is already assumed in the premise. For example: " God exists because this is what the bible says, and the bible is reliable because it is the word of God."

List of some other common fallacies in logic are as under:

1. The fallacy of appeal to authority

2. The straw man fallacy

3. The false dilemma fallacy

4. The bandwagon fallacy

5. The Texas sharpshooter fallacy

6. The correlation/causation fallacy

*The reader can read more on the topic of fallacies on the links given below. Some of the examples are taken from the links below:

1) https://philosophy.hku.hk/think/fallacy/list.php

2) https://blog.hubspot.com/marketing/common-logical-fallacies.----written by Karla Cook

Words of Wisdom

"Insults are the arguments employed by those who are in the wrong."
      ---Jean Jacques Rousseau

"Most couples have not had hundreds of arguments; they have had the same argument hundreds of times."
      -----Gay Hendricks

Technique 17: Make a Wager

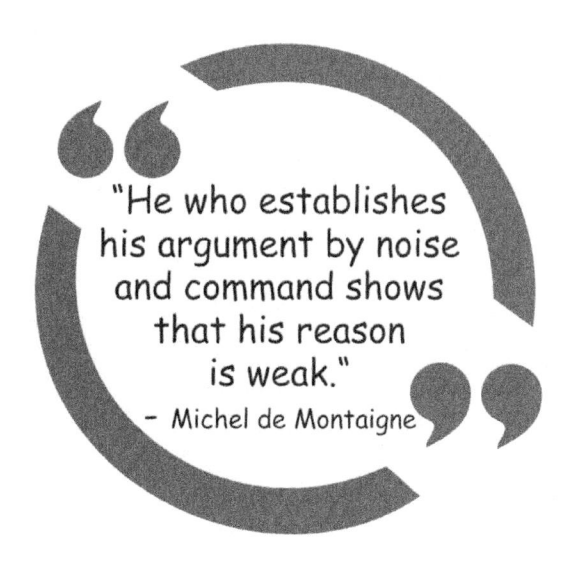

> "He who establishes his argument by noise and command shows that his reason is weak."
> – Michel de Montaigne

Short title :

In this technique, a wager(bet) is made by you to support your argument. When your opponent notices that you are willing to **put your money where your mouth is**, they usually back off, especially if they are not 100 percent sure of their argument. The quantum of wager usually decides the level of confidence.

Details Description:

This technique can be used under two circumstances. Either when you are **100 percent sure** of your submission or when **neither you** nor your **opponent is sure** of their respective submissions. In the second case, once you realize that your **opponent** is not sure and sounds doubtful, give a fatal blow to his argument by making a bet with him.

Example:
Situation: You and your cousin are having an argument on which is the oldest civilization in the world. You are saying it's Greek, and he is saying it's the Roman one. Both of you are not sure. You spot your **opponent**'s lack of confidence.

Your Cousin, "I am quite sure; it's the Roman civilization which is the oldest."

You, "No, it's Greek."

You again, "In fact, I bet a hundred bucks that it's Greek."

Analysis :

In the above example, the moment you notice that your **opponent** was doubtful (even though you may also be uncertain), you support your argument with money. This is a great way to win an argument psychologically. People usually **make a bet just for the sake of making it**. They are not serious about it most of the time. The bet is, in this case, only indicative of your **level of confidence**. Very few times, your **opponent** is going to turn back and take your bet. Also, you only made a bet when you noticed your **opponent's** lack of confidence. Backing your argument with money is a great way to keep your **opponent** quiet.

Words of Wisdom

"A true Englishman doesn't joke when he is talking about such a serious thing as a wager."

— *Jules Verne, Around the World in Eighty Days*

"All of life is a wager."
---*Christopher Hitchens*

"Every year, if not everyday we have to wager our salvation upon some prophecy based upon imperfect knowledge."
-----*Oliver Wendell Holmes Jr.*

"Belief is a wise wager. Granted that faith cannot be proved, what harm will come to you if you gamble on its truth, and it proves false? If you gain, you gain all; if you lose, you lose nothing. Wager, then, without hesitation, that He exists."
--- *Blaise Pascal*

Technique 18: Ask Questions

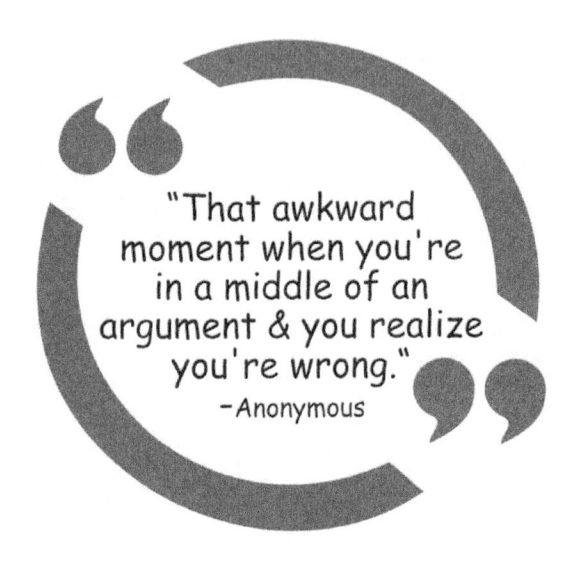

> "That awkward moment when you're in a middle of an argument & you realize you're wrong."
> – Anonymous

Short Description:

In this technique, your arguments are not statements **but questions** which the opponent cannot answer. Asking undefendable questions to your opponent is one of the best ways to win arguments.

Details Description:

Sometimes, the best way to win an argument is not to give any answers or explanations but to ask questions. The questions which you ask, **you**

already know their answers. Therefore, you are confident that your **opponent** will lose the argument if he attempts to answer your questions. Your questions are of such a nature that their possible answers are your explanation to your argument. However, instead of directly explaining, you chose to ask the right questions. There is an old adage, "**To get the right answer. You need to ask the right question**". Similarly, to win an argument, you need to ask the right questions.

If you give explanations, you put yourself in a 'justifying mode,' and it is a little weak position. People can easily argue with explanations and reasons, but when you ask questions the whole game changes. Again, it is a lot to do with psychology and how we humans communicate. I vehemently ask the reader to try this technique. You will be invincible if you can master this strategy.

Example:

Situation: Your driver has approached you for a raise in salary. You take excellent care of your driver. Never cut his salary even when he is late. Leave him early, when there is no work. Give him one month paid leave. Even after all this, he has come to you for a raise citing that your neighbor has raised his driver's salary. You know that your neighbor does not give perks as you do.

Your driver, "Sir, Mr. Jones, has increased the salary of his driver. I was hoping you will also."

You, "My dear Michael, tell me, Does Mr. Jones give his driver a month's paid leave?"

Your driver: (is silent as the answer is against him.)

You, "Everybody cuts half a day's salary when drivers are late. Have I ever cut your salary when you have been late?"

Driver: (quite)

You, "Sometimes, you go home early due to personal work. Have I ever stopped you or cut your salary?"

You, "Last year, when your son was ill. Did I not sponsor his medicines? Who does this much?"

Analysis

In the above-mentioned example, you have not got into an argument and explanation. You have not got into justifying your stand or giving lengthy explanations to your driver. You have said everything by just asking questions. This technique is a sure shot to winning arguments as the questions you ask, you already know the answers, and you also know that the answers are in your favor.

Words of Wisdom

"He who asks a question remains a fool for five minutes. He who does not ask remains a fool forever".
---proverb

"It is not the answer that enlightens but the question."
----Eugene Jonesco

"The art and science of asking questions is the source of all knowledge."
---Thomas Berger

"There is no stupid question: stupid people don't ask questions."
--Olivia

Technique 19: Majority Wins

> "There can be no progress without head-on confrontation."
> - Christopher Hitchens

Short title:

In this technique, you use the **power of numbers** to your advantage. If you are in a group where more people support your viewpoint, then take a hand count to support your argument.

Details Description:

This technique can be used when you are in a **big group,** and the **majority of the people** support your view. In such situations, it does not matter who is factual right or wrong, but what matters is how many people support a particular perspective.

Logically, just because more people believe in a particular thing doesn't mean that it is right. Also, sometimes the group is such that it may belong to a specific cult, religious belief, culture, or organization which may believe in a particular ideology. In such situations, one can take the **support of numbers** to win an argument. It is a human response that when more people support something it is seen to be right. In other words, **Majority Wins**.

Example:
Situation: Millions of people have morning walkers groups. Every morning, they walk and talk in that group and discuss topics ranging from politics to pollution. These groups are also notorious for having heated arguments. So, you are part of a large morning walkers group where in an argument, you are taking a particular stand, and another person is taking the opposite. However, you notice that most people in the group support your perspective.

You, "Guns should be banned. Civilians should not be allowed to own guns. The risk of civilians owning guns far outweighs its benefits."

Your friend, "No, I think guns give a person a sense of security, and it is the constitutional right of every person to defend himself."
You, "Mr. ABC, what do you have to say about it?"

You, "Mr. XYZ, what are your views?"

You, "Mrs. ZZZ, do you agree with me?"

All of the three people agree with you, and you use the power of numbers to defeat your Opponent.

Analysis

Even though the merits and demerits of an argument should **not be weighed** by the number of people supporting it or against it, in real practical life people always tend to get influenced by numbers. If the **majority agrees** to a particular view, opponents to that view become a little weak and ultimately give up their argument if they don't have enough courage. Use this strategy effectively if you find most people supporting your view.

***Once again a polite reminder.** The reader is requested not to get into the merits and demerits of the argument. The illustration is only for understanding the technique.

Words of Wisdom

"One man with courage makes a majority."
----Andrew Jackson

"There is nothing uglier than an unrighteous and foolish majority."
----Mehmet Murat ildan

"Whenever you find yourself on the side of the majority, it is time to pause and reflect."
----Mark twain

Technique 20: Self Deprecation and Sarcastic Laughter

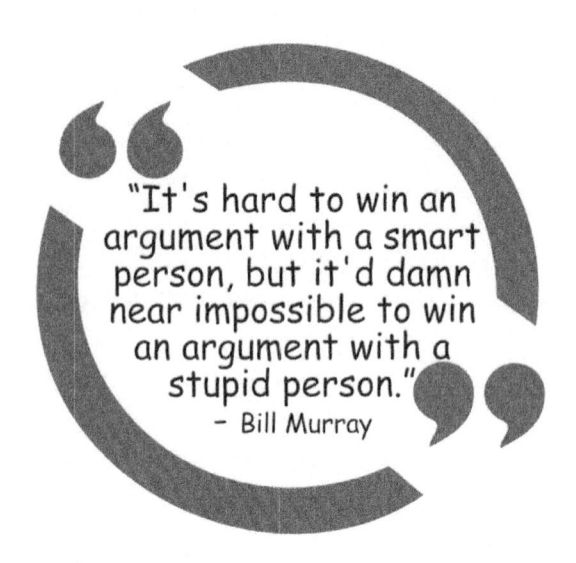

> "It's hard to win an argument with a smart person, but it'd damn near impossible to win an argument with a stupid person."
> – Bill Murray

Short Description:

In this technique, you use two weapons/tools namely 1) Self Deprecation 2) Sarcastic Laughter, either **individually or in conjunct** , depending on the situation to counter the aggressive attack of your **opponent** which you feel is completely unjustified/unreasonable/unwarranted or bizarre.

Tool 1: Self Deprecation

If your **opponent** is aggressively attacking you, and you think that the attack is not worth defending as it is **unwarranted or unreasonable**, start to **agree** with your **opponent's** allegations sarcastically. Once you begin to agree, you **take away the power from your opponent**. You self-deprecate to take away the **control** from your **opponent**. Self-deprecation requires guts, but if you can do it, it is an effective way to thwart a scathing attack on you or your views.

Details Description:

There are some situations where your **opponent** fiercely attacks you or your views. If the attacks have some bases or are relevant, you can even think of countering them. Still, sometimes the attack is so **silly** and unwarranted that you don't want to stoop down to the level of defending or countering your **opponent's** attacks. Your opponent has power over you only **till the time you disagree** with him and counter-attack him. Nevertheless, if you **agree with him (even sarcastically**), you take away the power from him, because he has nothing more to say. How can your **opponent** counter you when you agree with him?

Your self-deprecation has to be in a **sarcastic manner** so that your agreement is also like a **disagreement.** The operative word here is '**sarcastic.**'

It is important to reiterate that your opponent gets his power from your **non-acceptance,**

disagreement, and resistance. If you agree, your **opponent** has no power over you.

Example:
Situation: You are an employee/Journalist of a TV channel and you are interviewing a controversial personality. This personality is supposed to have a bad temper, and he uses fear to attack people and get his way around. You are asking him important questions which he is unable to answer satisfactorily. This personality is getting angry because you are succeeding in cornering him with your sharp questions.

You, "So, Mr. X, you agree that you were responsible for initiating the crowd to burn the whole township down just because they did not allow your dog to wander around there?"

Mr. X, (to you) "You are a biased, manipulative, and unfair person. Your questions are misplaced, and you are asking the same purposely to increase the ratings and viewership of your channel. Journalists like you need to be hanged. You people have killed democracy."

You, **"Yes, Yes, I am unfair and manipulative.** I agree with you, Sir. **In fact, maybe I am the most manipulative person in the world.** However, I would appreciate it if you could answer some of the questions I have raised against you and answer them."

Analysis :

In the above example, by self-deprecating yourself, you **have taken power away from your Opponent**. Now, your Opponent cannot continue his attack on you because you have agreed with him. If you had countered it or disapproved of his allegations, your Opponent would have an opportunity to argue further and prove his point. But once you have agreed, there is **no occasion for your Opponent to continue.**

Tool 2: Sarcastic Laughter

In this tool, **sarcastic laughter** is used as a **tool to neutralize the argument** of the **opponent** without getting into an actual argument. If the argument of the **opponent** is so **absurd** that it is against human intelligence, then there is hardly any possibility that you will be able to win the argument because you cannot argue against a silly or bizarre and ridiculous argument. In such cases, laughter does two things. First, It prevents you from **falling into a trap of** arguing against something ridiculous. Then, it also sends a message to the **opponent** of what you think of that person's argument. **You kill two birds with one stone.**

Details Description :

It takes all kinds of people to make the world go around. There are millions of people floating on this earth who have extremely **low IQ** and who can never **appeal to reason**. Their whole purpose of existence on earth is to irritate others. These people create arguments out of nothing and make suggestions that leave you speechless and make you **question the intelligence of the human species**. These people speak and argue such bizarre things that even getting into an argument with them is an **insult to human intelligence**. In fact, if you get into an argument with them, you may land up pulling your own hair or even get physically violent because you can't tolerate the **stupidity of these people**. In such situations, when these people make their bizarre arguments, don't counter-argue. Just laugh. Let your laughter be **sarcastic**. But don't talk, just laugh. Laughter is the best and the only antidote against silly and low IQ people.

You can't beat an unreasonable, low IQ, and stupid person in an argument. They will never understand your amazing logic. And you will never be able to understand their infinite stupidity.

Example :
Situation: The world is at a standstill due to the outbreak of the coronavirus. You are the head of a big pharma company that is fighting against time to make a vaccine and cure people. You have been

called for a tv debate on how to solve the corona problem. One of the participants in this tv debate is a leader and a minister from a poor state. He is illiterate, but he became a leader due to vote bank democracy. He has also been called to give his two bits on how he plans to eradicate corona from his state.

The illiterate leader, "We are arranging a grand get together where we are going to shout, "Go away, Corona, Go away." We believe that by shouting this loudly, the coronavirus will completely go away."

The anchor of the show asks you, "What are your perspectives on the views expressed by the leader?"

You: "Just laugh, and laugh."

The Anchor(to you), "Sir, would you like to say something?"

You, "No, I cannot argue against the respected leader's logic(sarcastically), and you continue to laugh and laugh."

Analysis :

In the above example, the suggestion of the illiterate leader is so bizarre and farfetched that it would be foolish even to attempt an argument against the leader's suggestion. In such a situation, you should just laugh and laugh. Let the laugh be sarcastic, no problem. But don't argue against such a bizarre argument, because whatever you do or whatever you say, you will never be able to stoop down to the stupidity of your **opponent**, and if you try, **he** has more experience at that level, and he will beat you hollow.

Tools 1 and 2 can both be used effectively together, in conjunction, in complement, depending on the situation, to counter any unwarranted and bizarre attacks. The underlying tone of this technique is **"Sarcasm"**.

Words of Wisdom

"**Never argue against a stupid person. You will always lose.**"

"Two things are infinite: the universe and human stupidity; and I'm not sure about the universe."
— Albert Einstein

"Be who you are and say what you feel because those who mind don't matter and those who matter don't mind."
-----Bernard M. Baruch

"Be yourself; everyone else is already taken."

---Oscar wild

"To be yourself in a world that is constantly trying to make you something else is the greatest accomplishment."

---Ralph Waldo Emerson

YOUR RATINGS AND REVIEW MATTER

Now that you have completed reading the book, I request you to go ahead and give your valuable rating and review.

If this book was useful to you and you were able to learn something new or you were able to apply some of the techniques successfully or you liked anything about this book then my humble request is that you write a review so that it can help and benefit the future readers.

I want to change the world through words and communication. I need your help to reach out to as many people as possible.

For an author, there is no greater and better return than a testimonial.

Please click the link below to leave a testimonial:

https://amzn.to/2JnPljy

Also, if you want to contact the author or give any kind of feedback, please feel free to write on : connect@vishal-gupta.com

EPILOGUE

Even though the knowledge and technique of winning arguments is a powerful life skill to have, then also, it is recommended that one should avoid arguments as much as possible.

One should not win arguments at the expense of friendship or relations.

The tongue is the most dangerous thing in the world. Physical wounds can heal, but the wounds inflicted by the tongue sometimes last forever.

Knowledge is power. When to use a particular kind of knowledge is very important, and even what is more important is the wisdom of when not to use it.

I strongly advise the reader to use the knowledge learned from this book with great discretion and care.

I hope all readers gain something out of it and will benefit from the humble knowledge I shared.

VISHAL GUPTA

Acknowledgments

We cannot do everything ourselves. We all need relatives and friends and well-wishers, who support us and believe in us.

I thank, from the bottom of my heart, all the people mentioned below for supporting me, believing in me, and for giving their precious time to me so that I could give the best to this book. THANK YOU!

(Alphabetical wise) :-Aalok Mehta, Aniket Phule, Deepa Shah, Dilip Ahuja, Harina Pawar, Ibrahim Bohra, Jiya Gupta, Krati Gupta, Prabodh Agarwal, Reena Rupani, Saurabh Jain, Samir Agarwal, Siddhanth Jain, Som Bathla, Vyom Gupta.

"**A moment of gratitude makes a difference in your attitude.**"
—Bruce Wilkinson

"**Gratitude is not only the greatest of virtues but the parent of all others.**"
—Cicero

"Appreciation is a wonderful thing. It makes what is excellent in others belong to us as well."

—Voltaire

"I can no other answer make but thanks, and thanks, and ever thanks."

– William Shakespeare

"Acknowledging the good that you already have in your life is the foundation for all abundance."

– Eckhart Tolle

Dedication

This book is dedicated to my father, **Shri Vinod Kumar Gupta**, with whom I have spent hundreds of hours arguing and ultimately losing.

I LOVE YOU, DAD, FOR WHATEVER YOU TAUGHT ME.

DISCLAIMER

Although the publisher and the author have made every effort to ensure that the information in this book was correct at press time and while this publication is designed to provide accurate information regarding the subject matter covered, the publisher and the author assume no responsibility for errors, inaccuracies, omissions, or any other inconsistencies herein and hereby disclaim any liability to any party for any loss, damage, or disruption caused by errors or omissions, whether such errors or omissions result from negligence, accident, or any other cause.

The ideas, procedures, and suggestions contained in this book are not intended as a substitute for consulting with an expert.

Neither the author nor the publisher shall be liable or responsible for any loss or damage allegedly arising from any information or suggestion in this book.

Names, characters, and incidents in this book are either the products of the author's imagination or used in a fictitious manner. Any resemblance to an actual person, living or dead, or actual events is purely coincidental.

COPYRIGHT © 2020 VISHAL GUPTA

All rights reserved. No part of this book may be reproduced or transmitted in any form or by any means, electronic or mechanical, without written permission from the author, except for the inclusion of brief quotations in a review. For permission to quote or for bulk orders, please contact the author. The author can be contacted at:

    vishalchief@gmail.com

    connect@vishal-gupta.com

    Mobile : +91- 9820308218

vishalgupta

Printed in Great Britain
by Amazon